Animal
Coloring Book
For Adults

relaxing and meditation

Jose Rodriguez

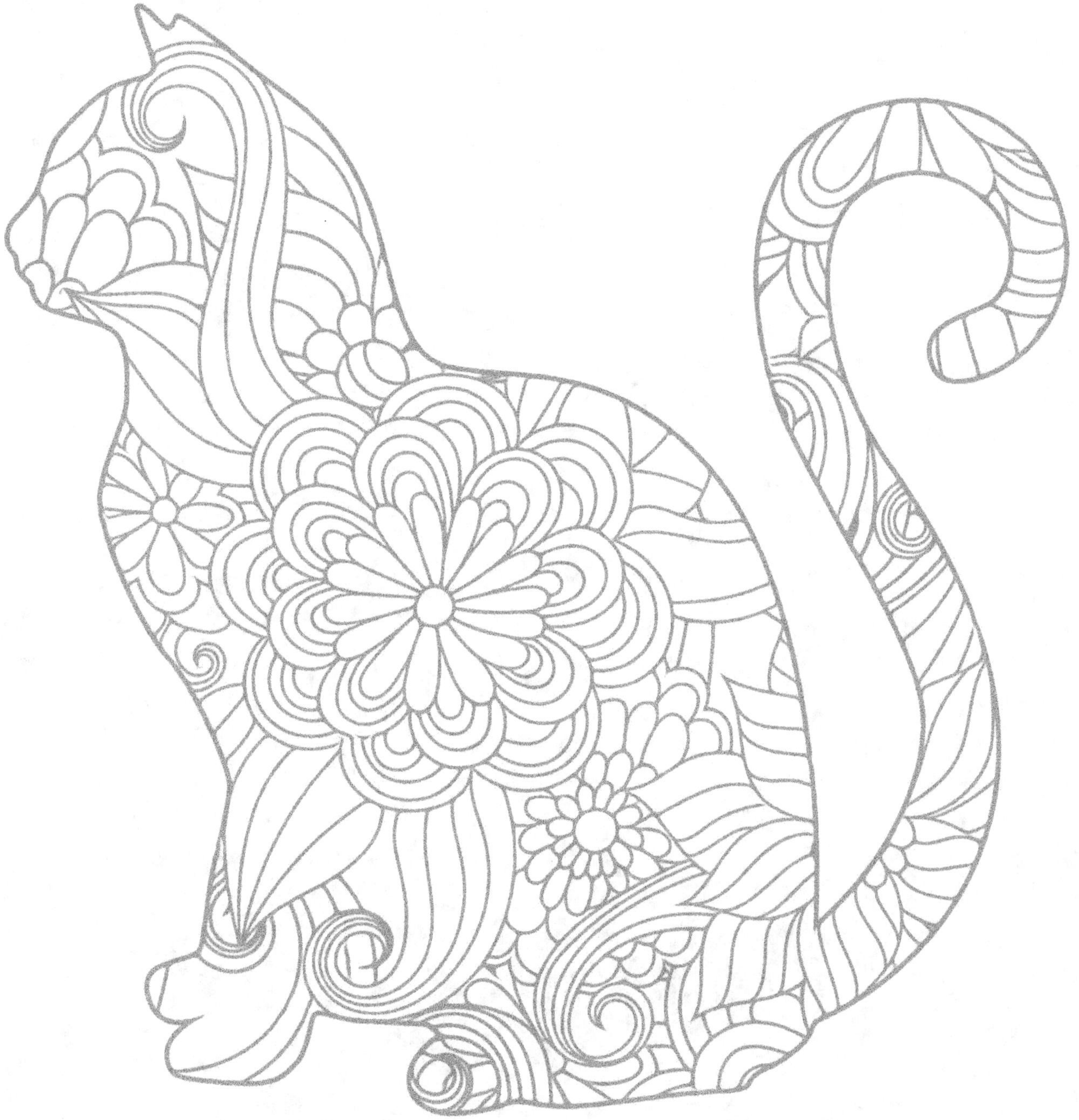

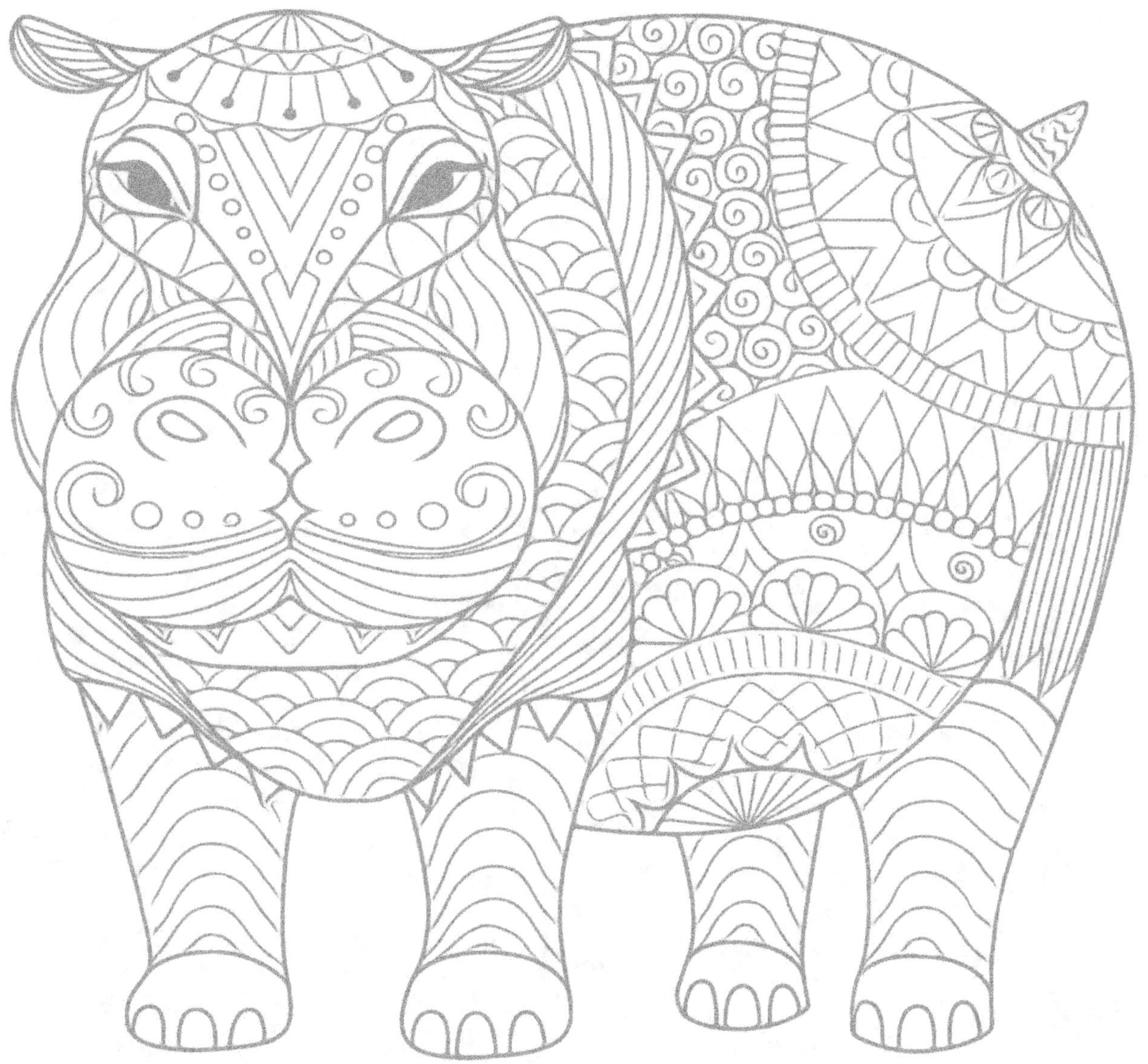

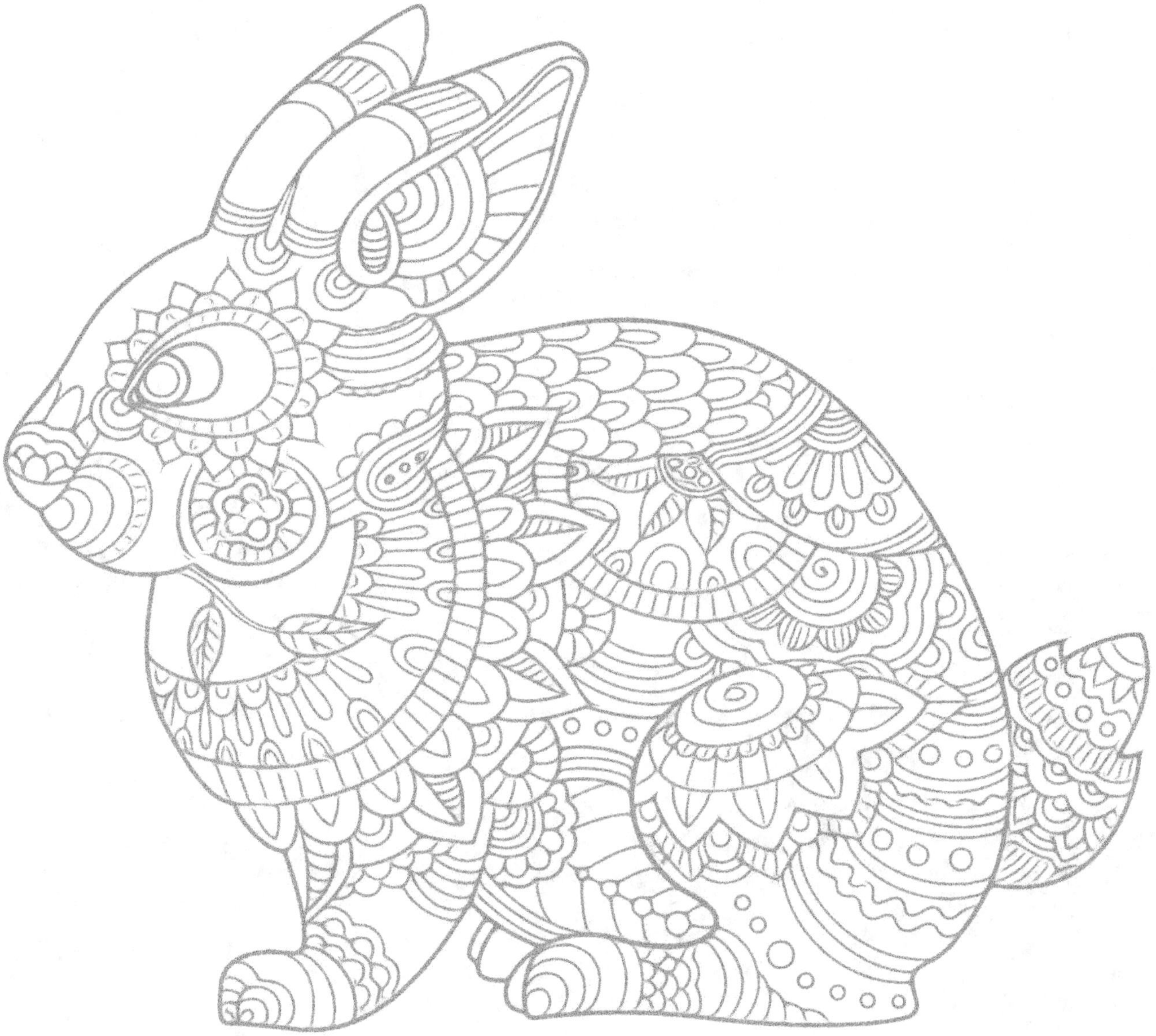

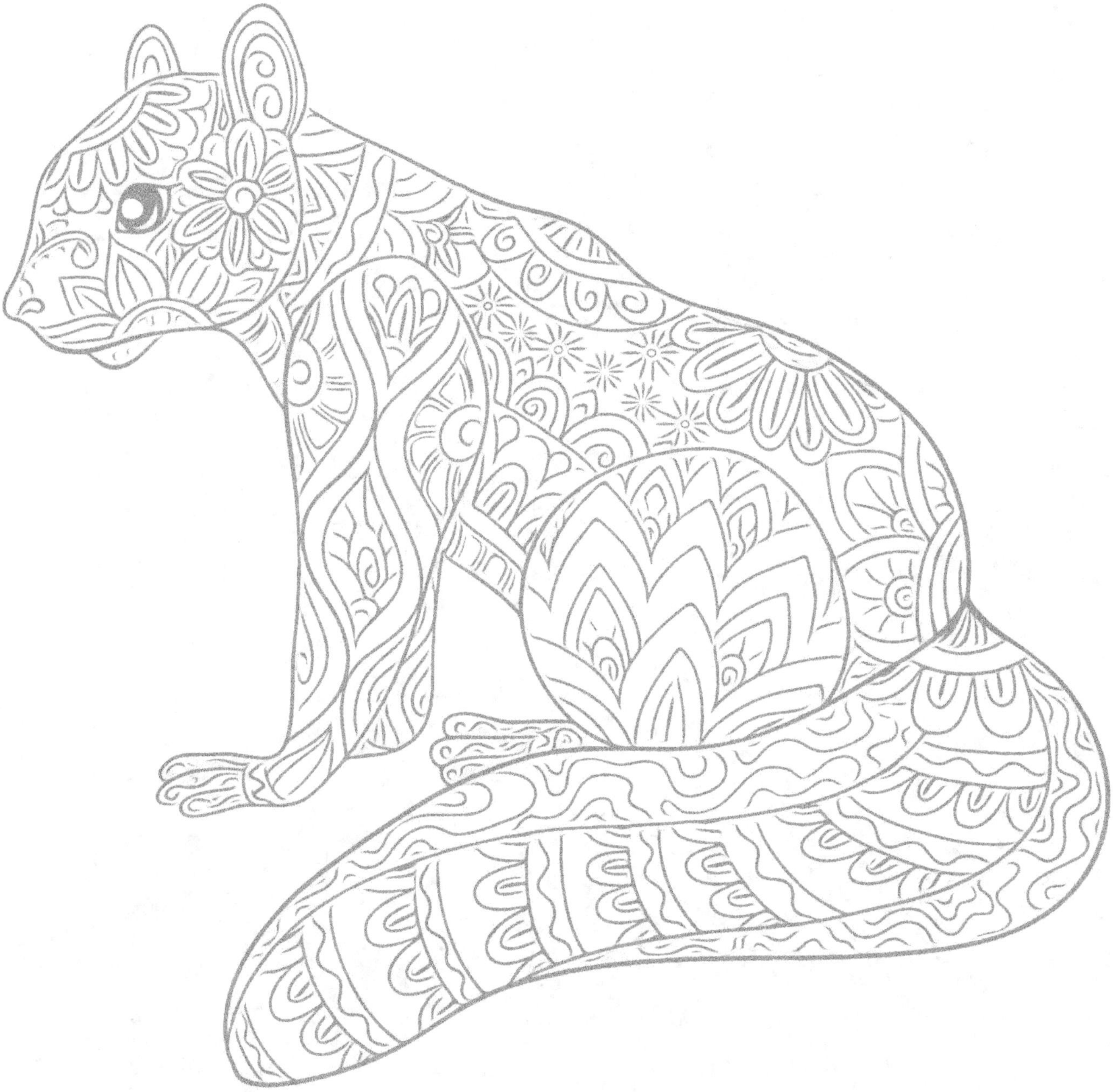

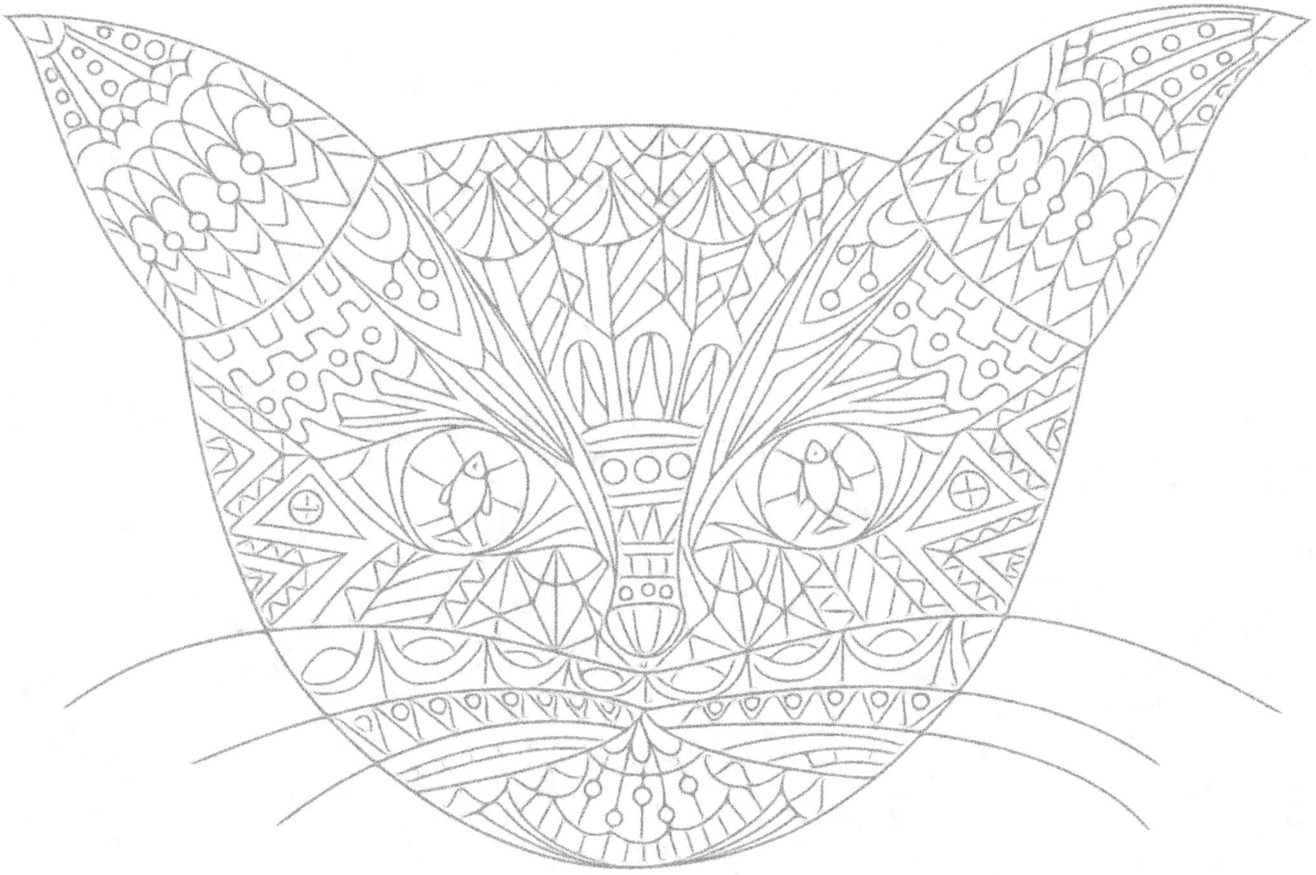

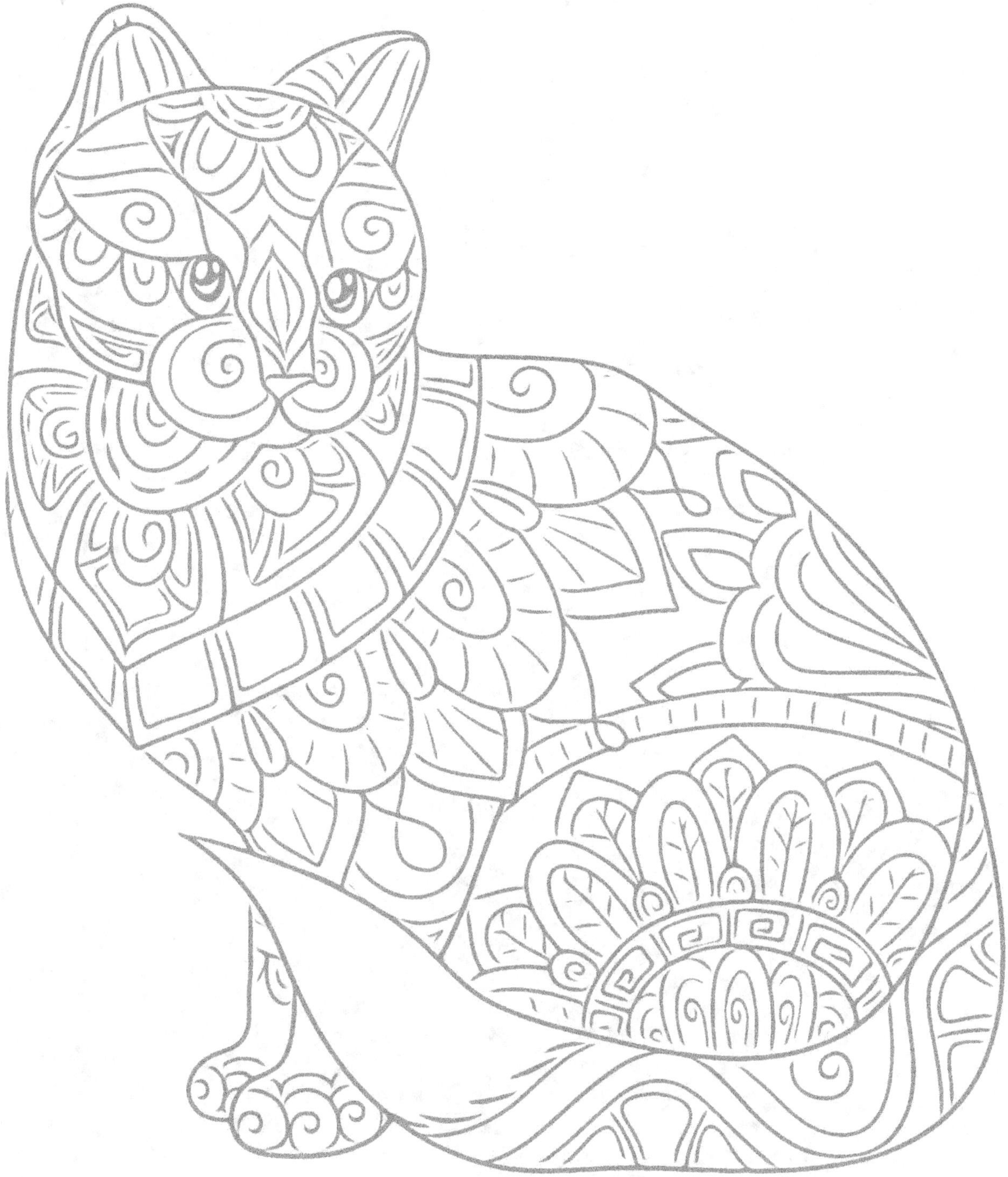

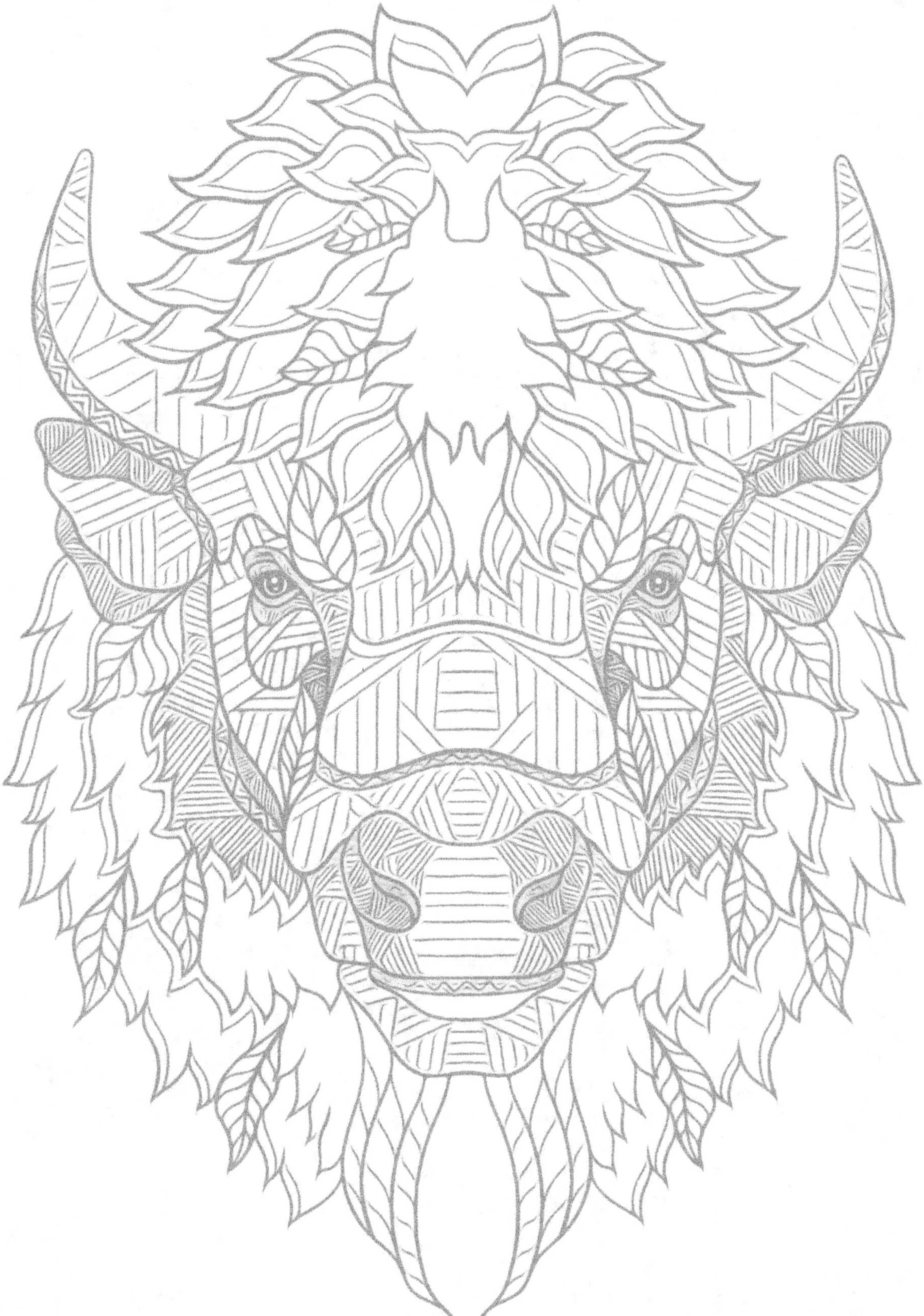

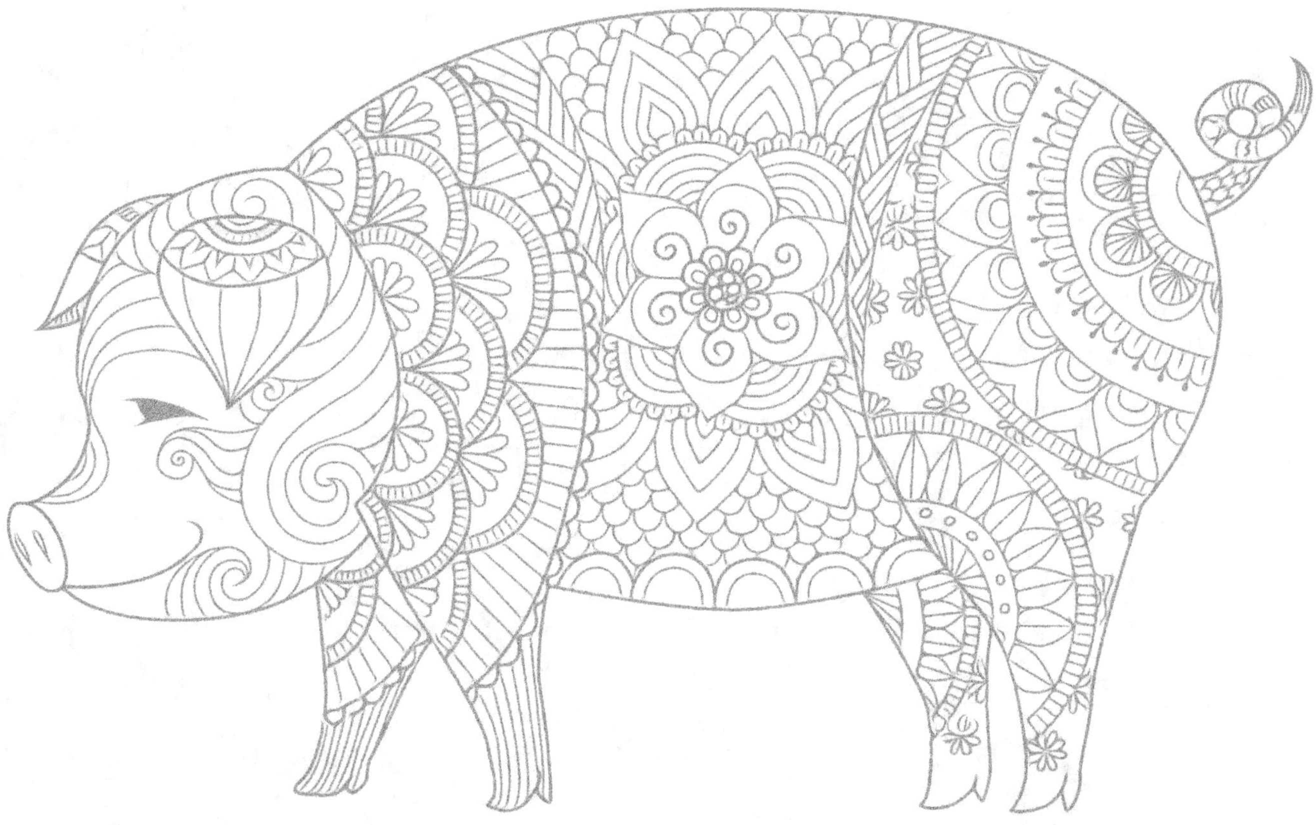

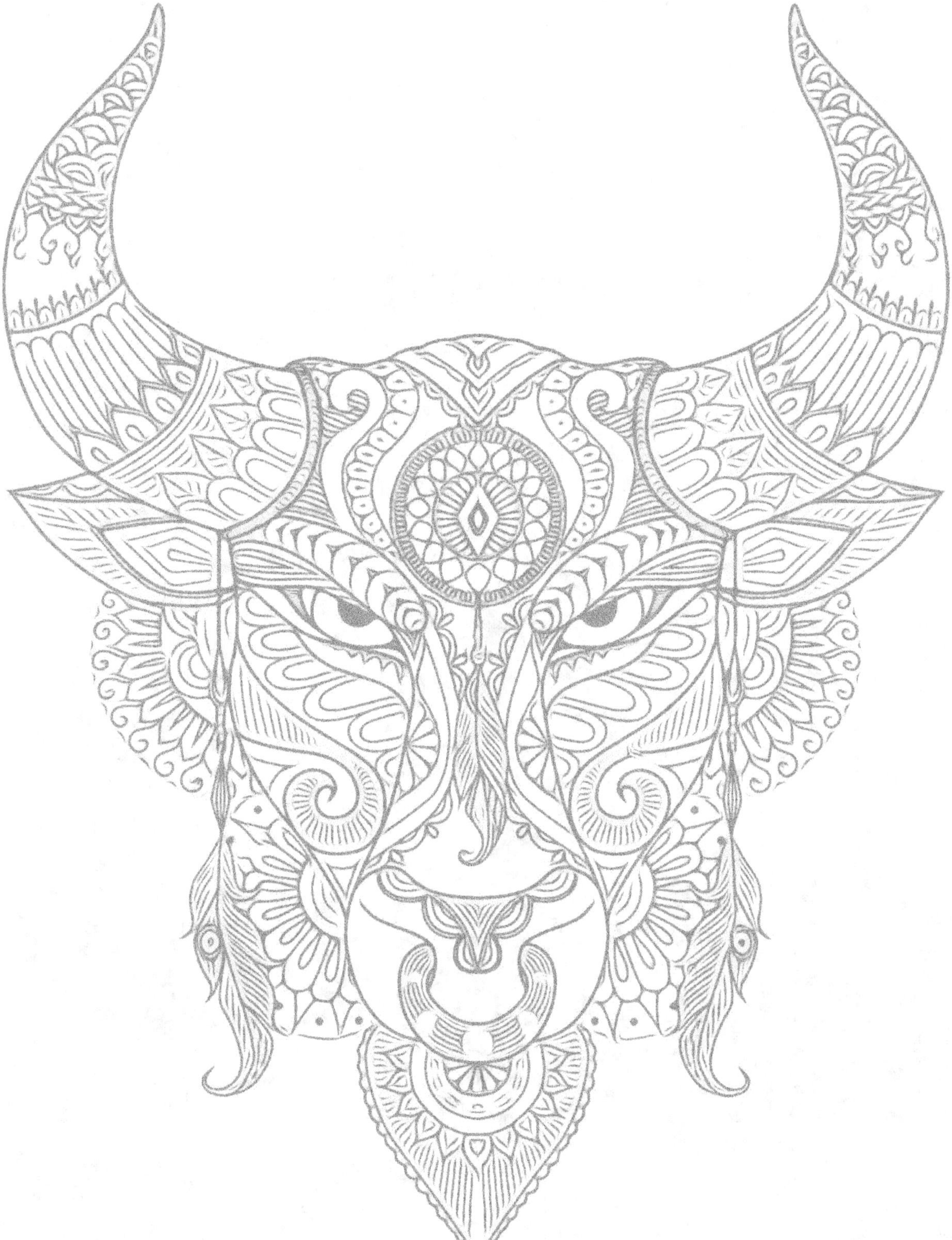

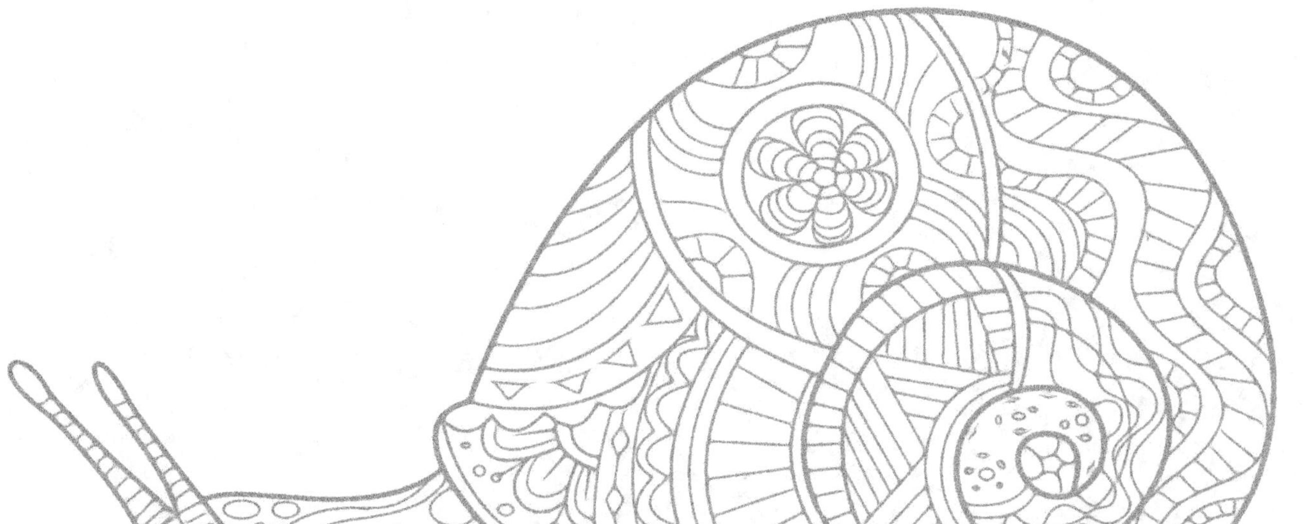

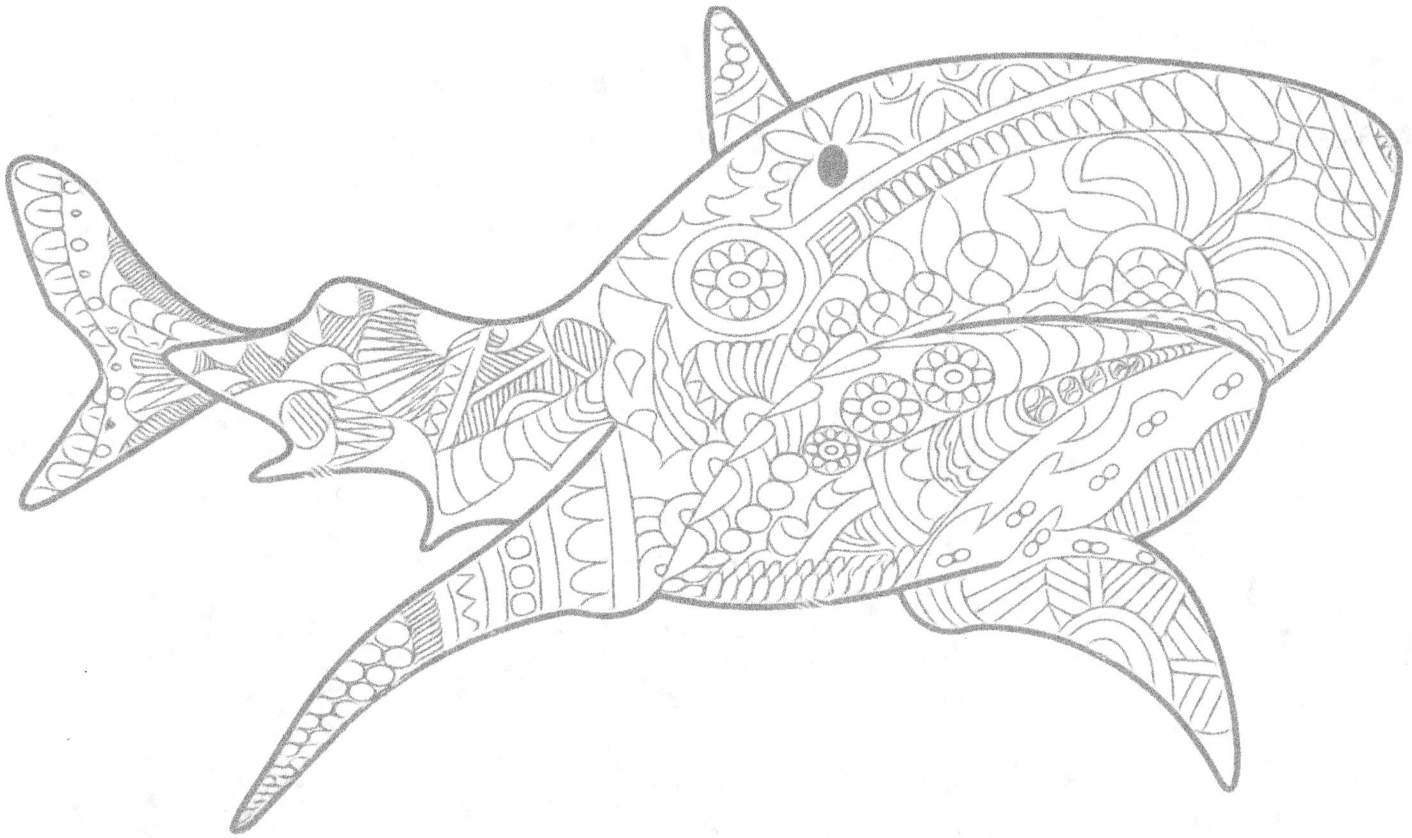

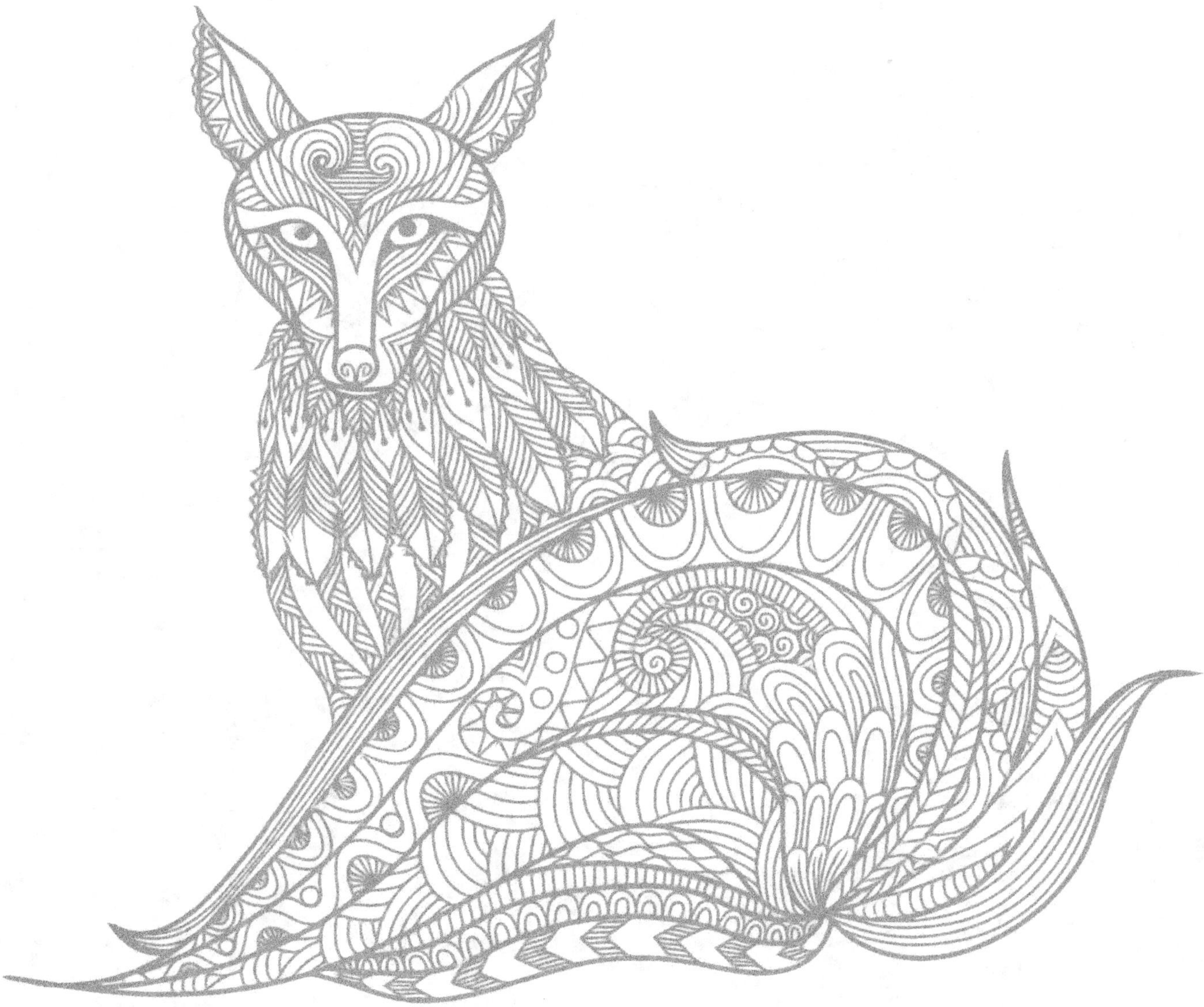

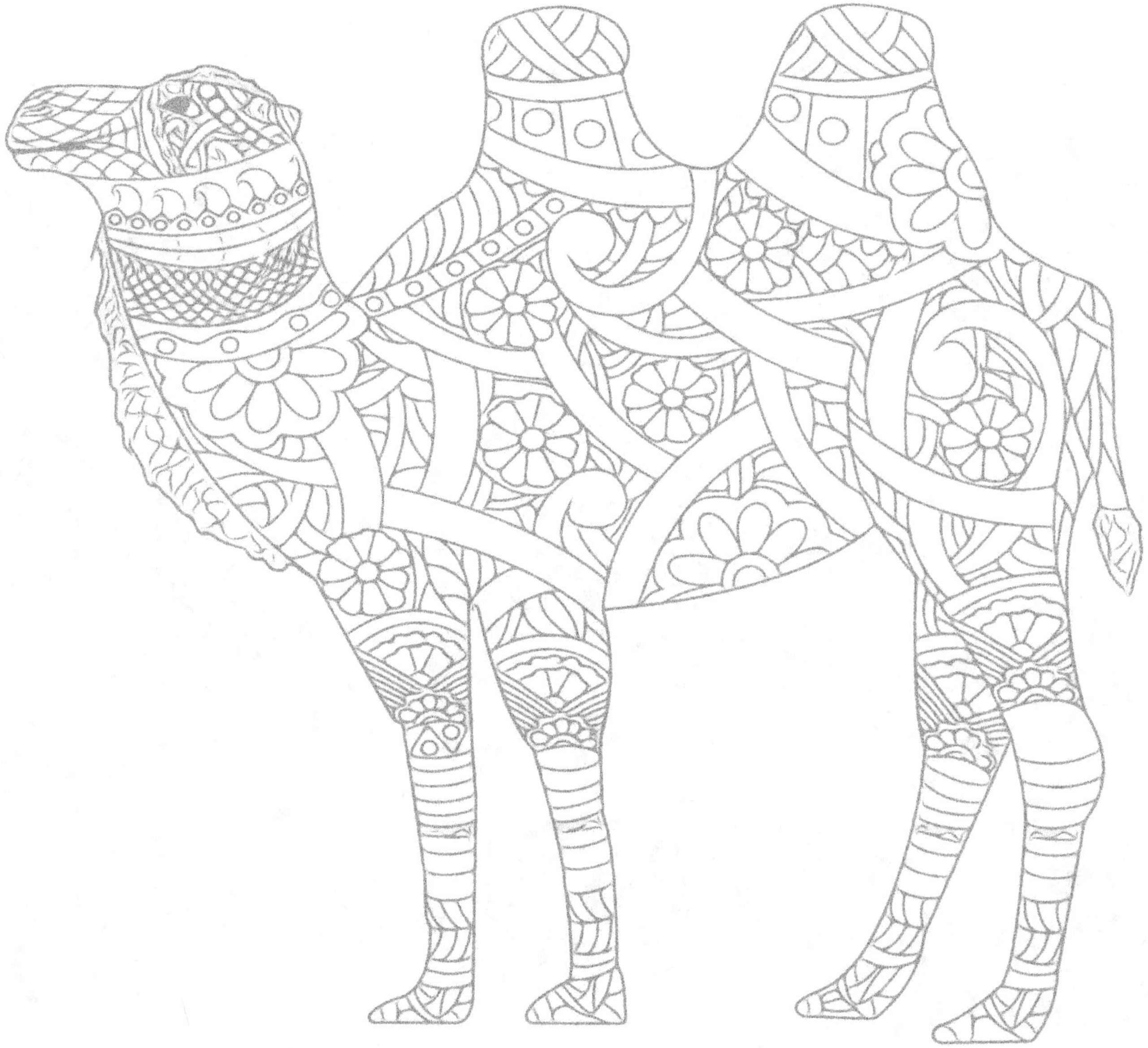

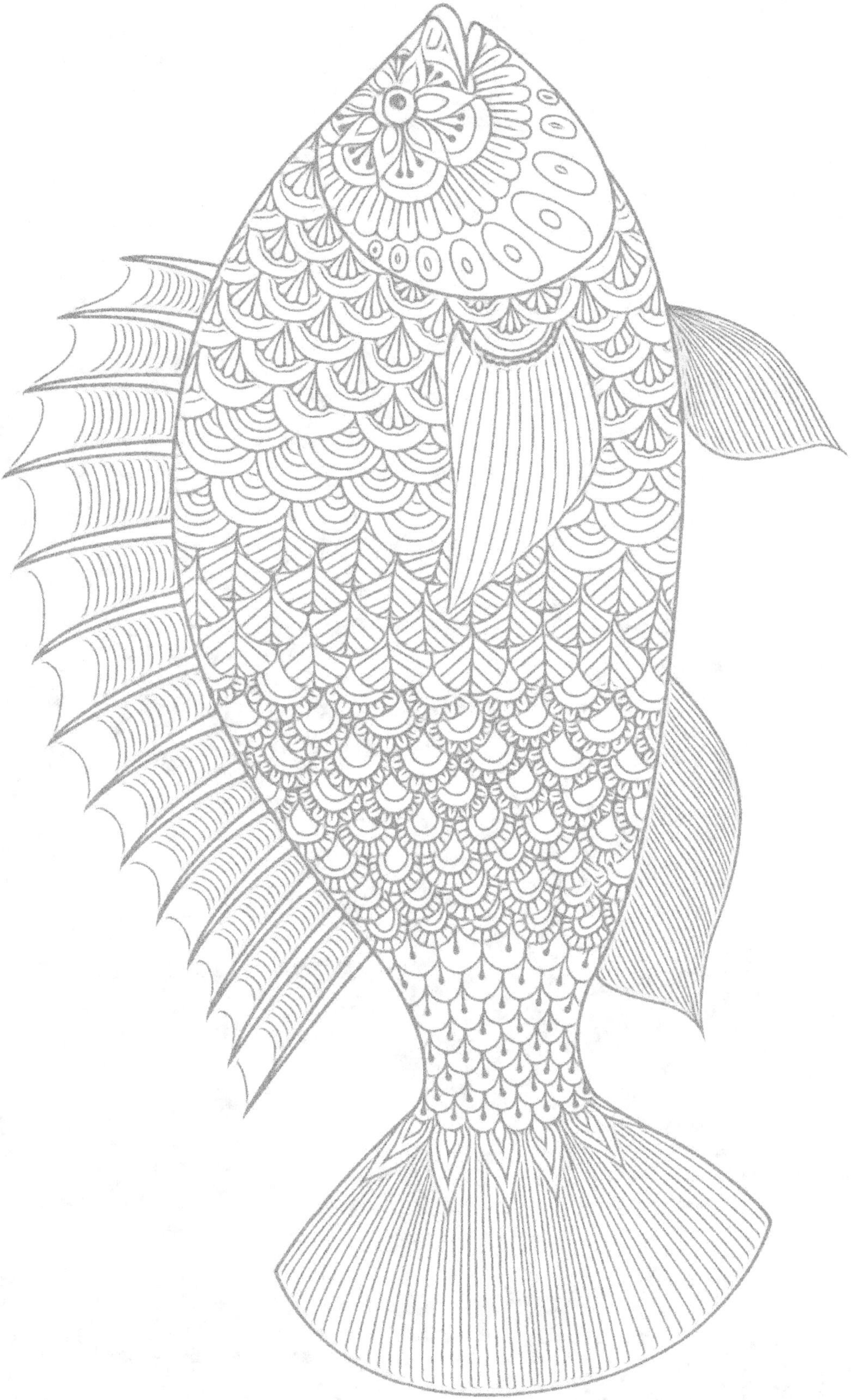

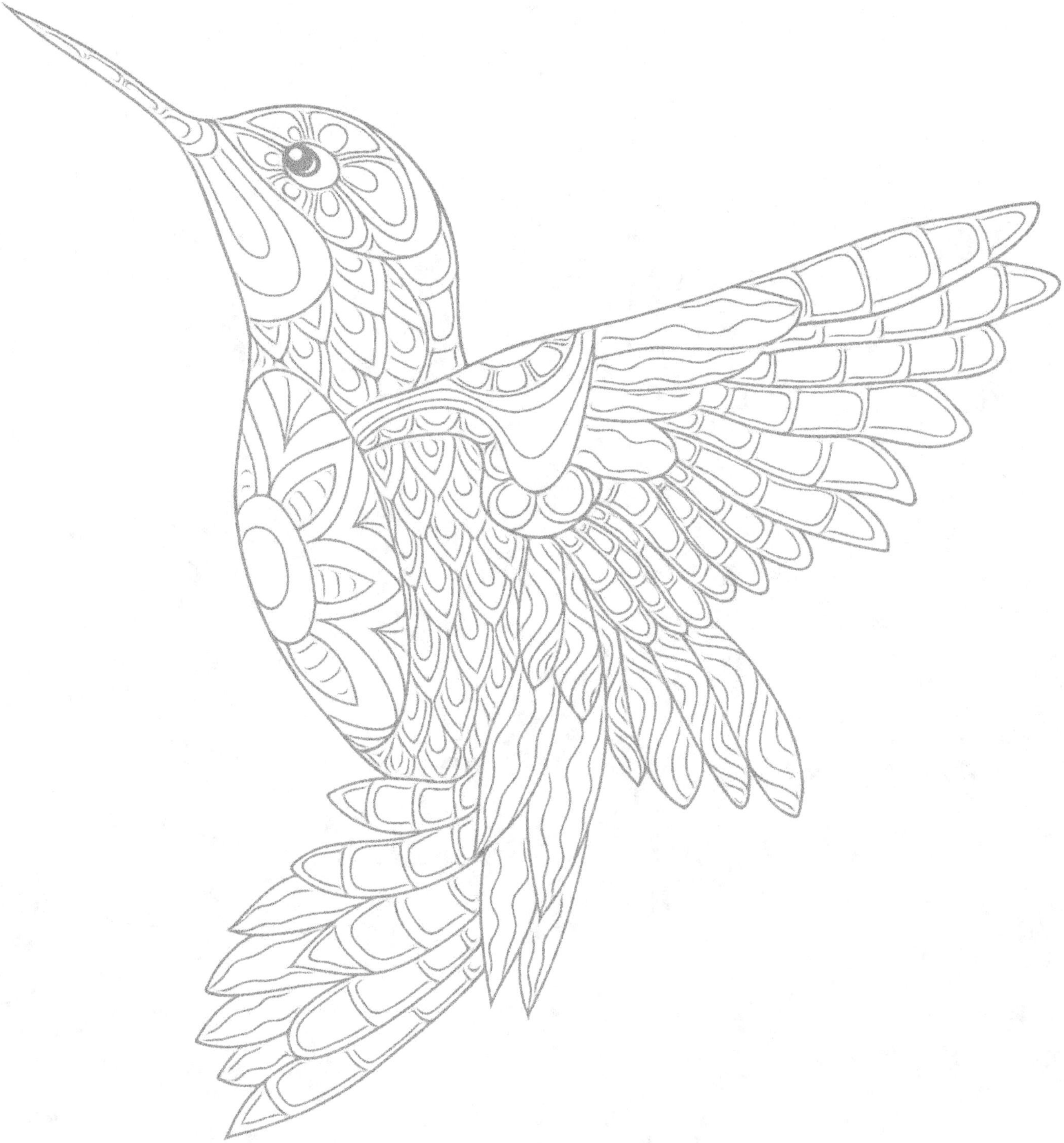

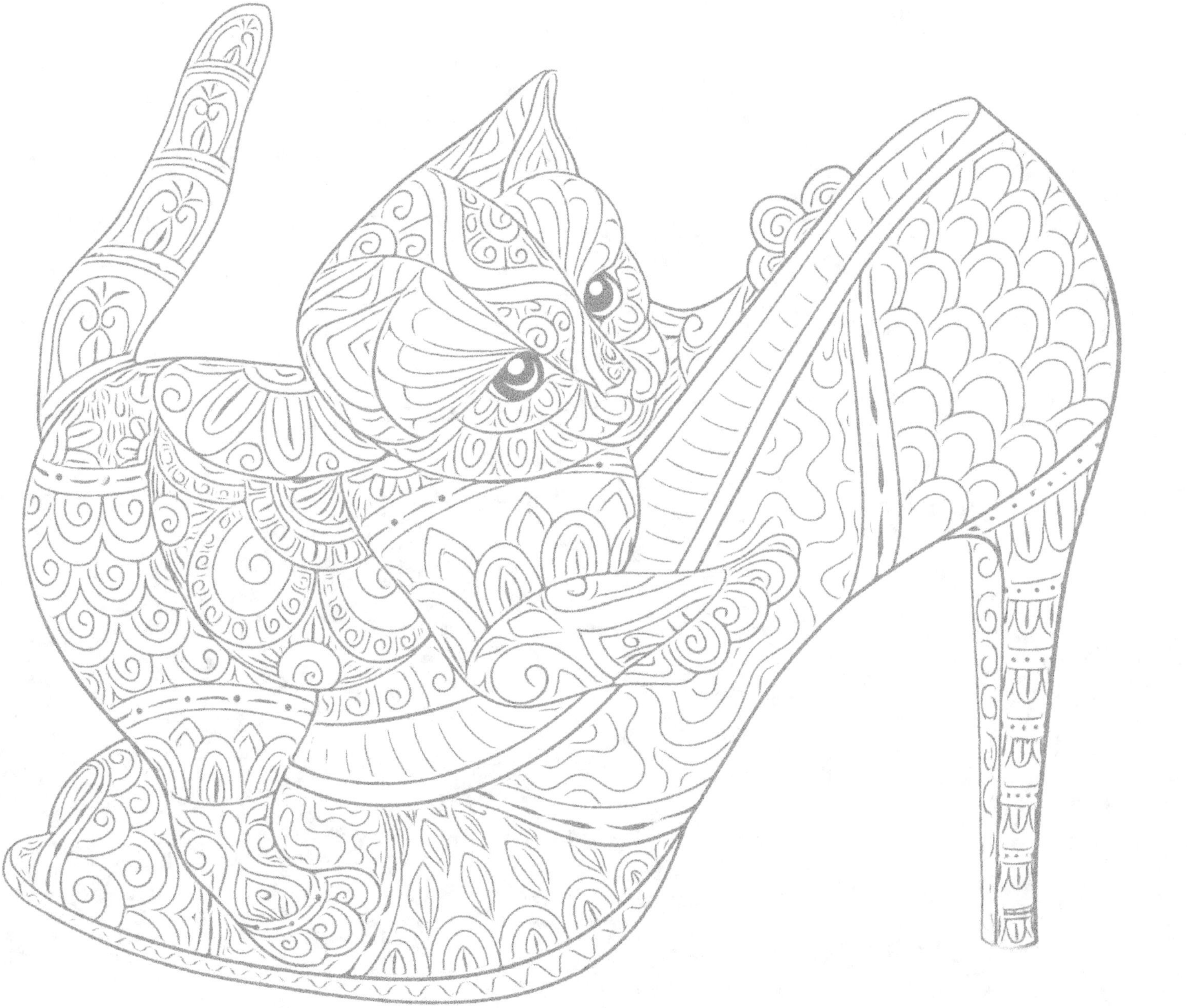

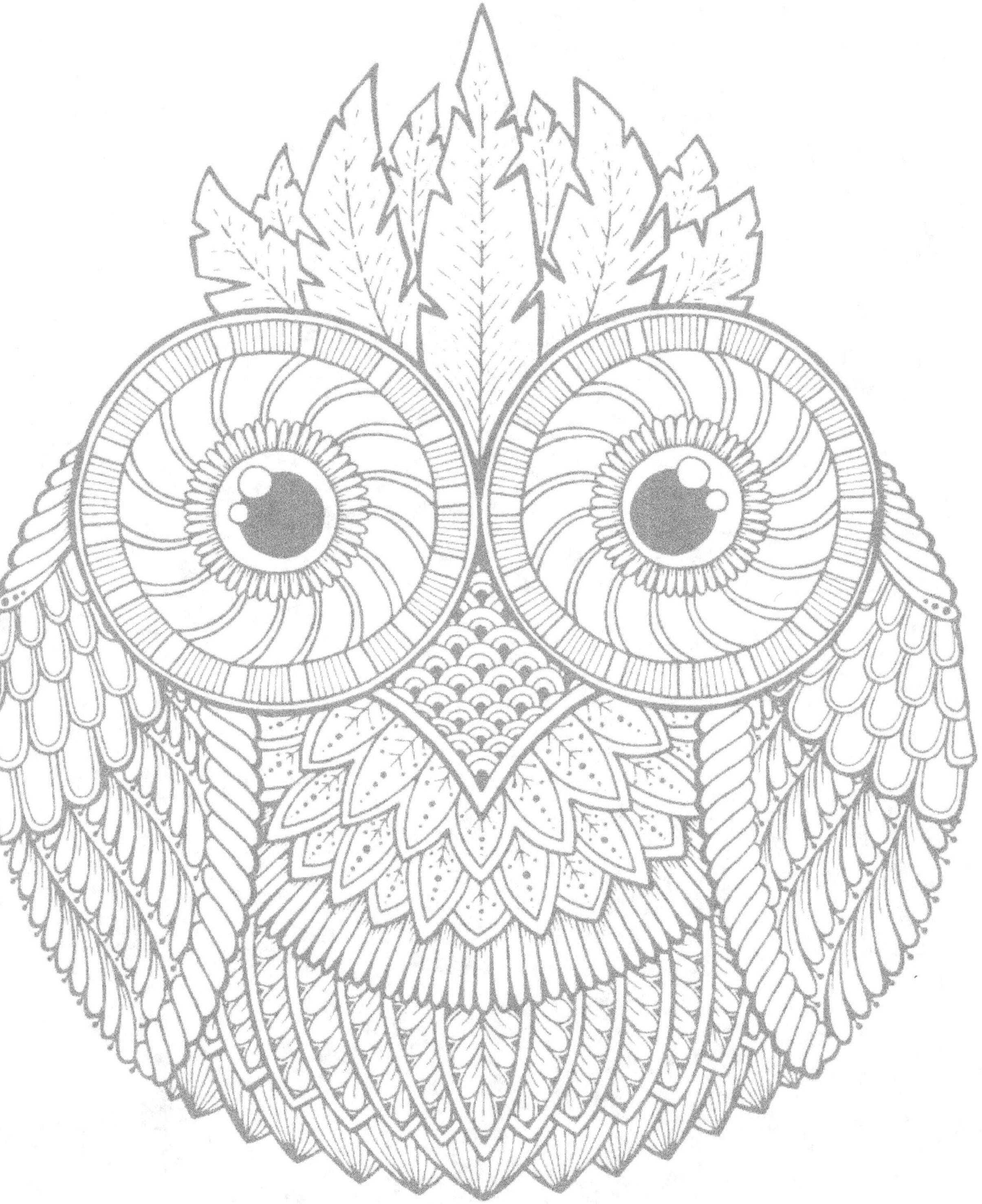

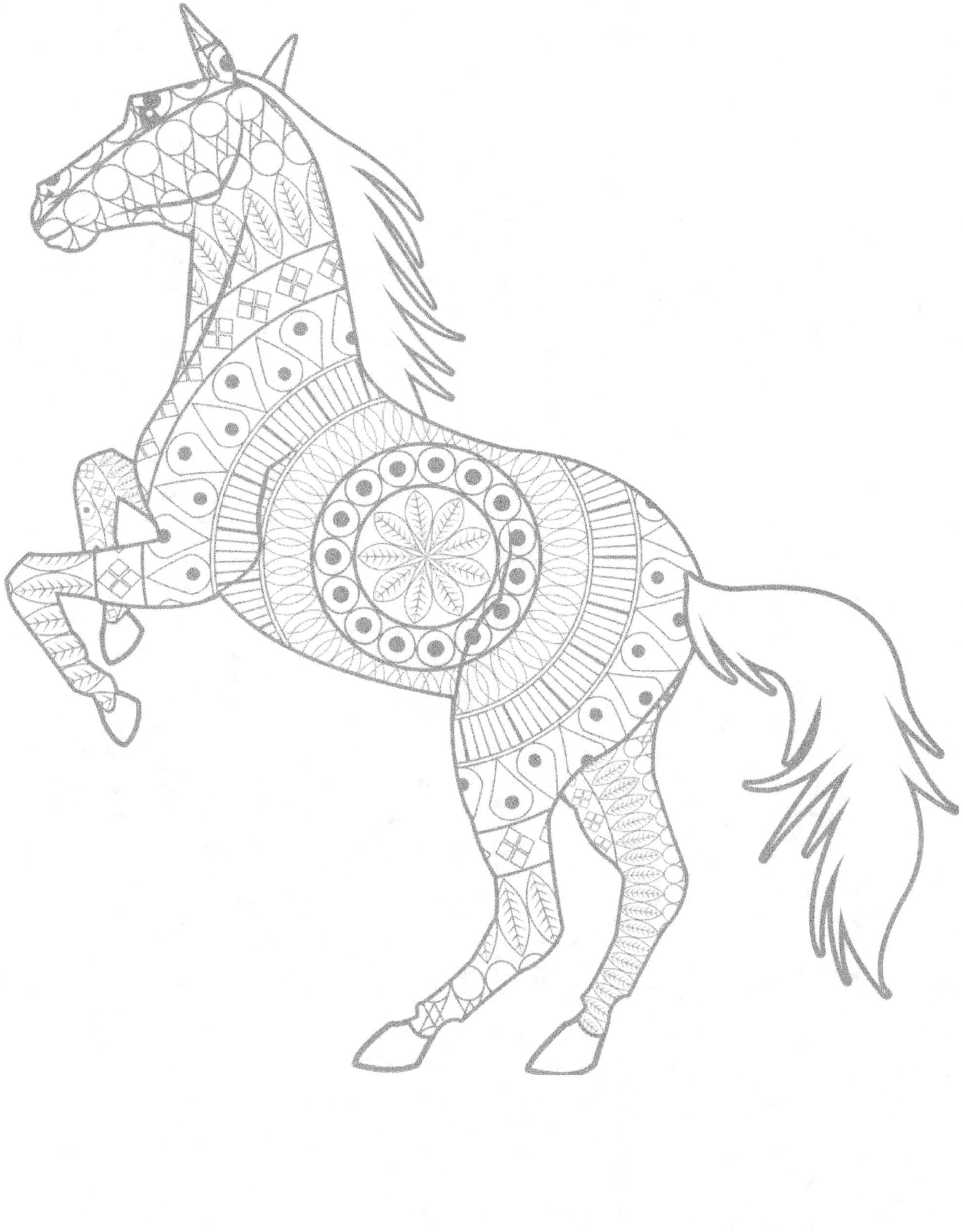

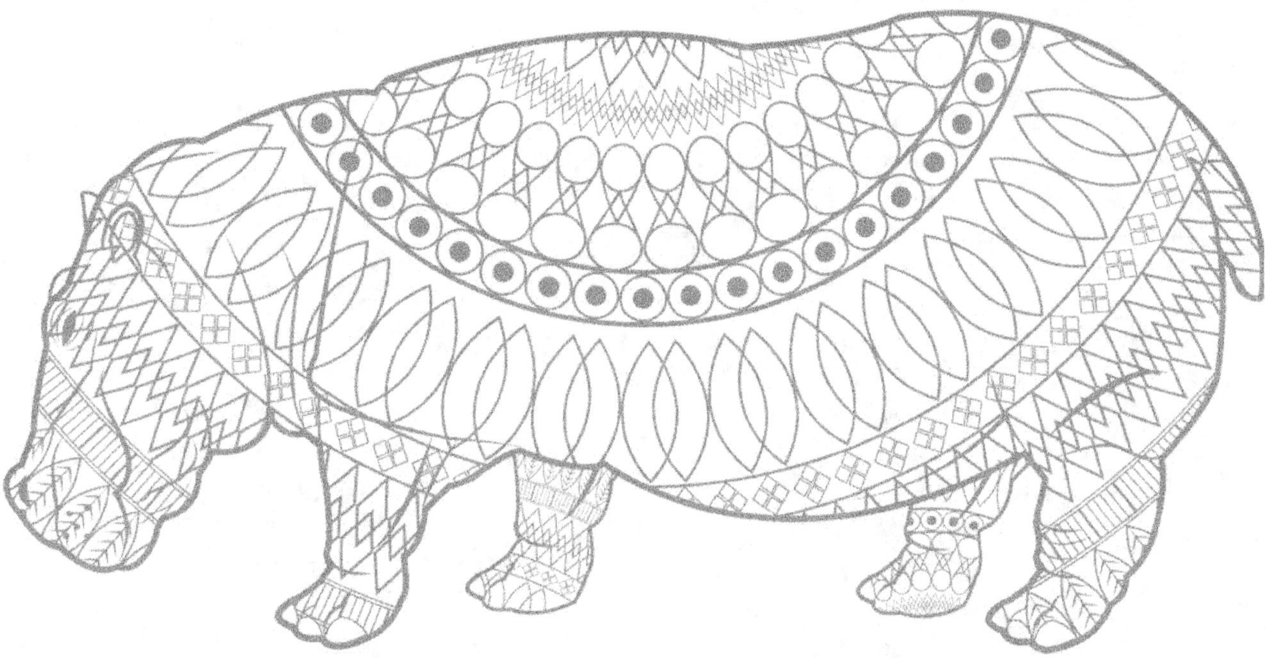

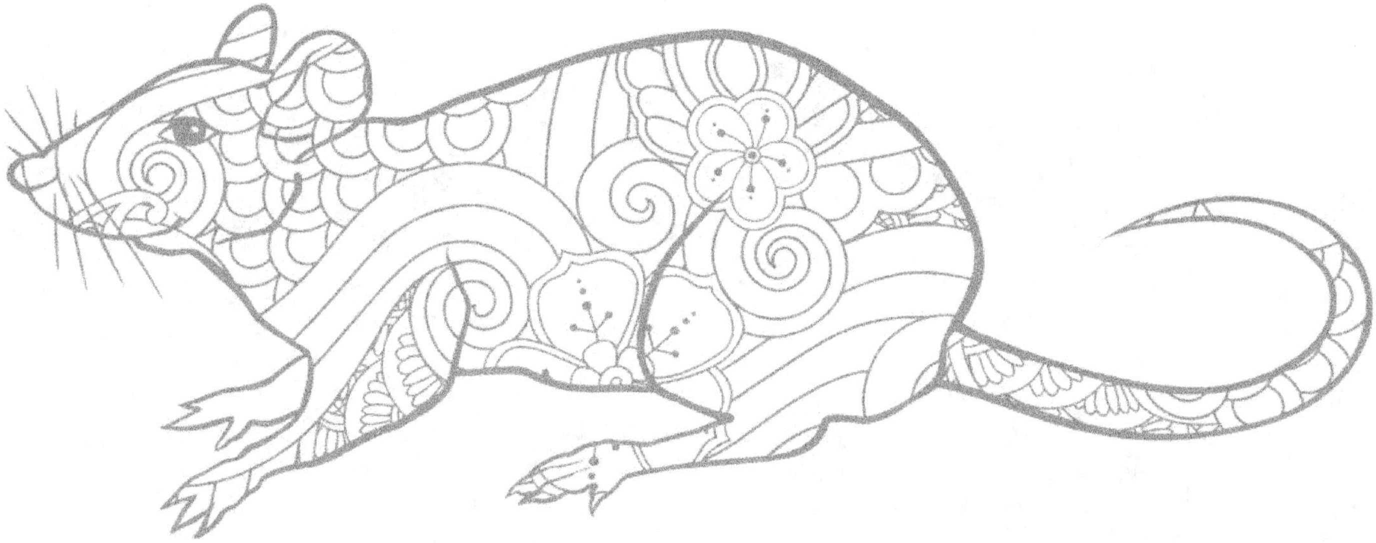

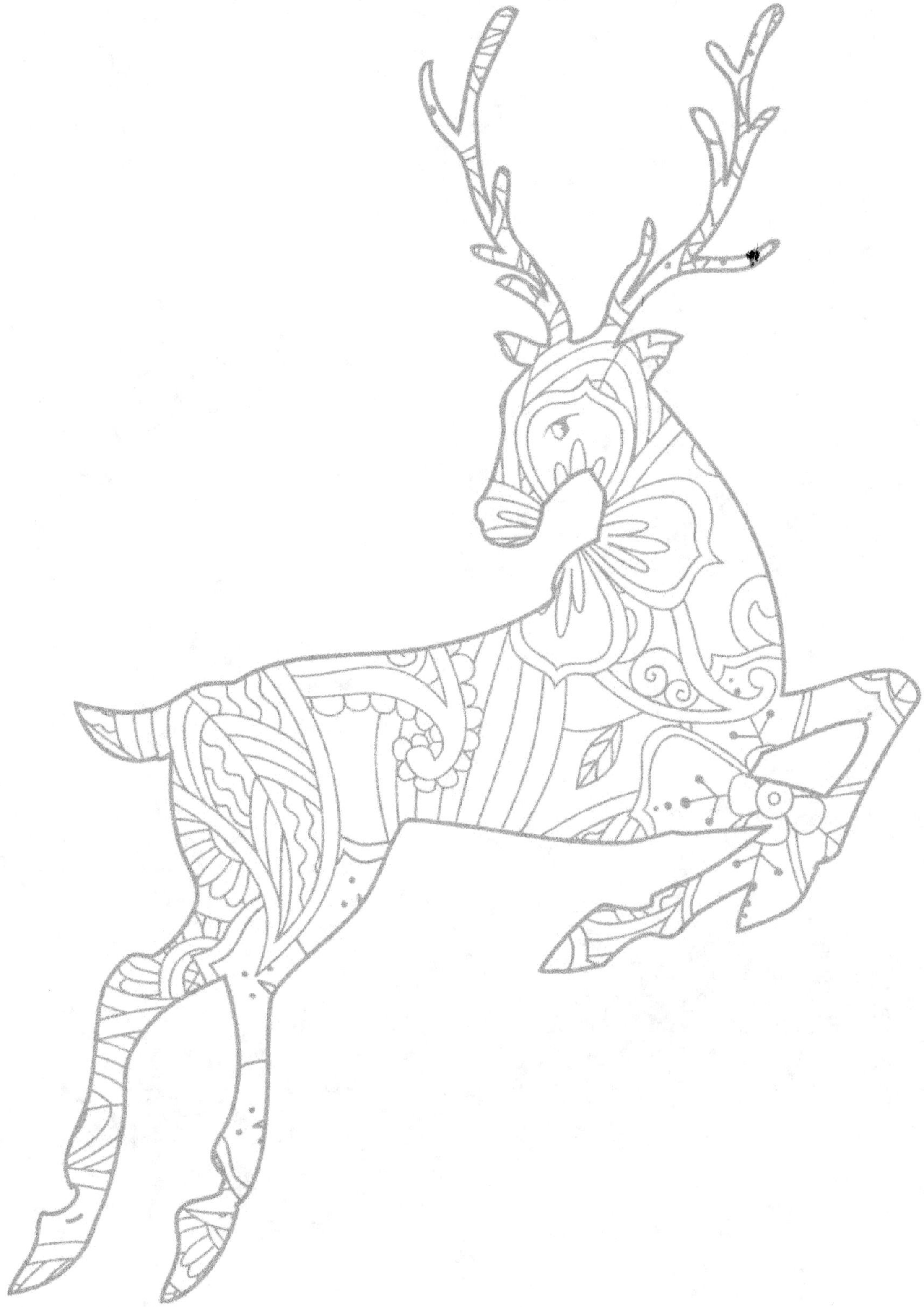

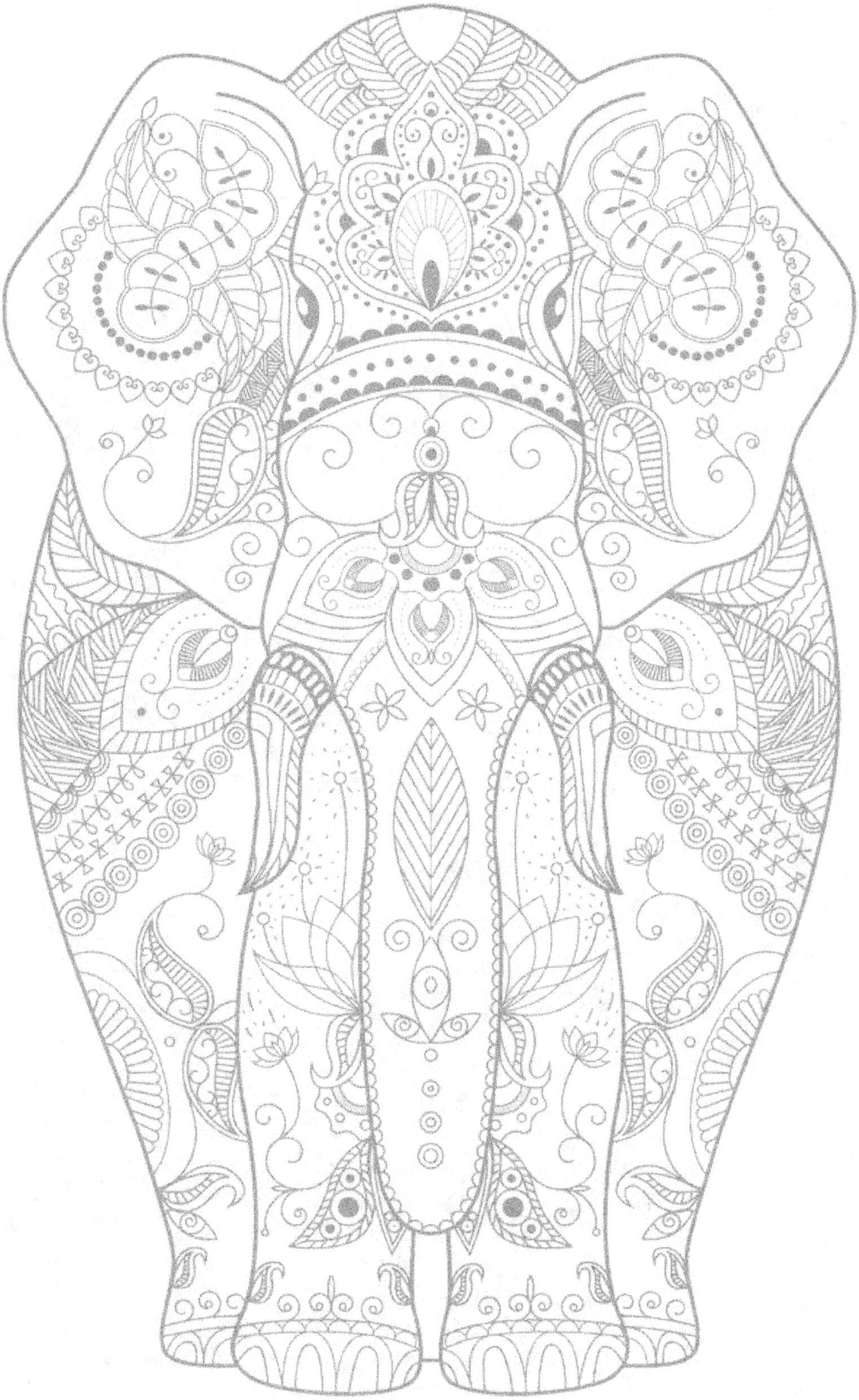

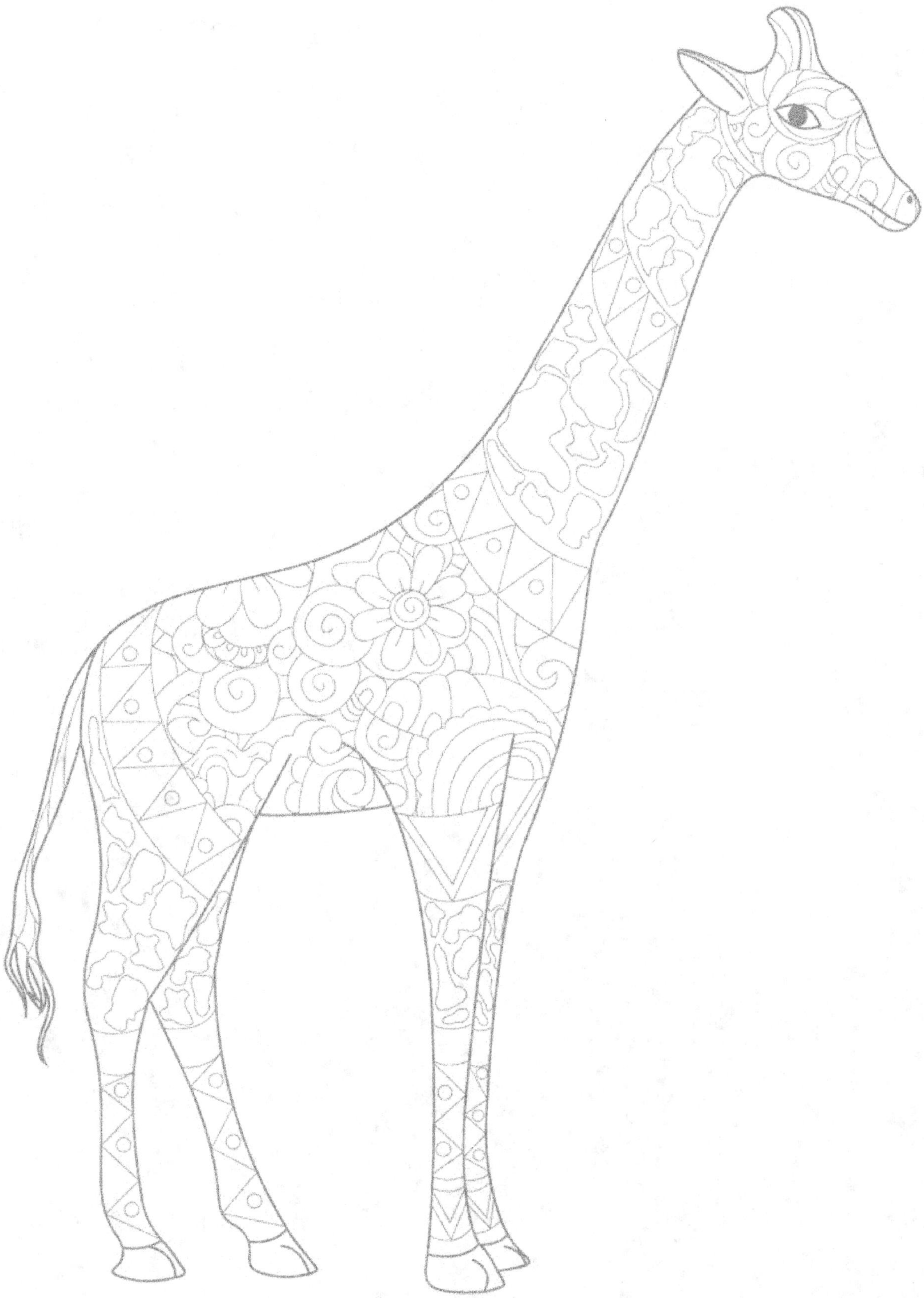

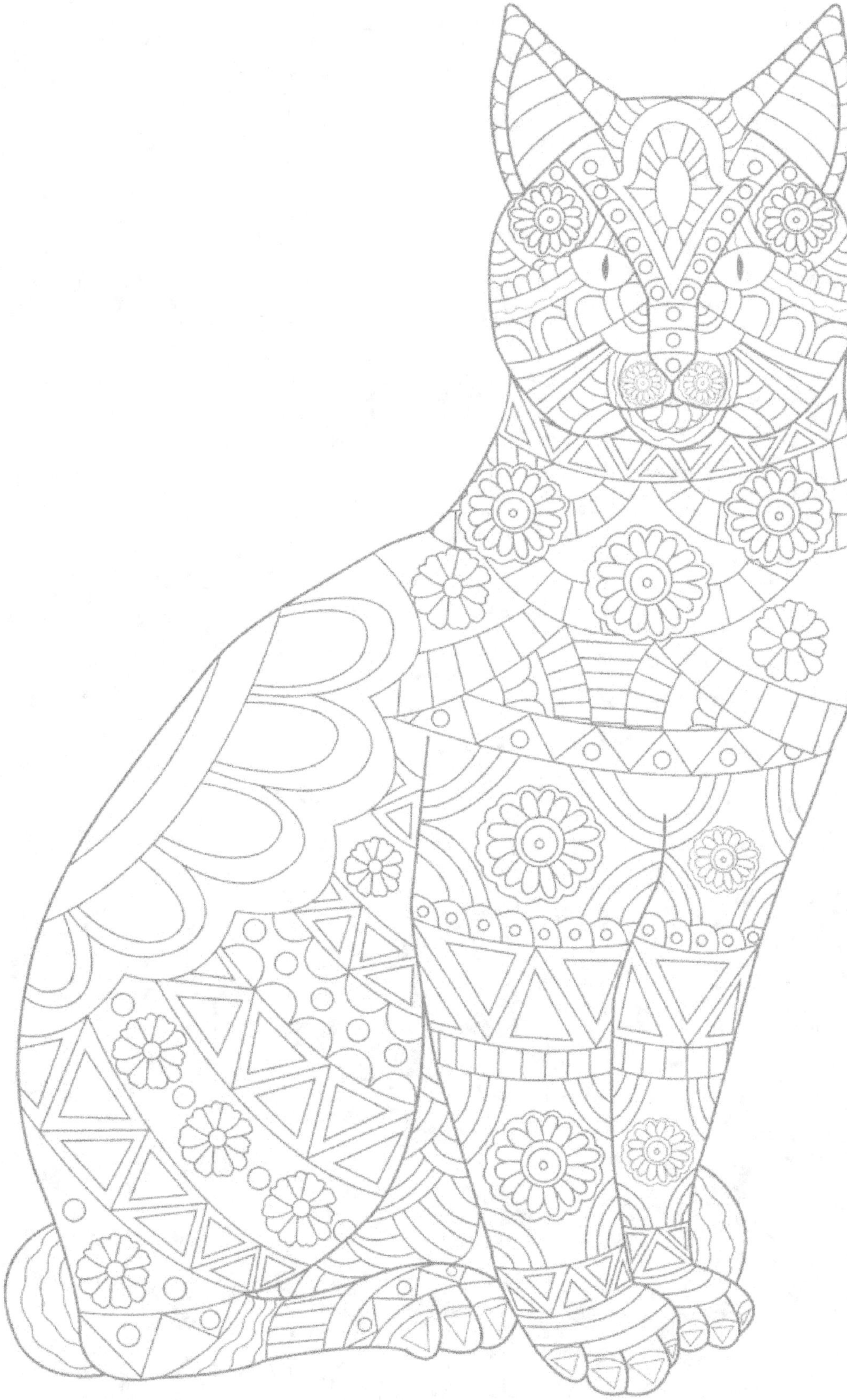

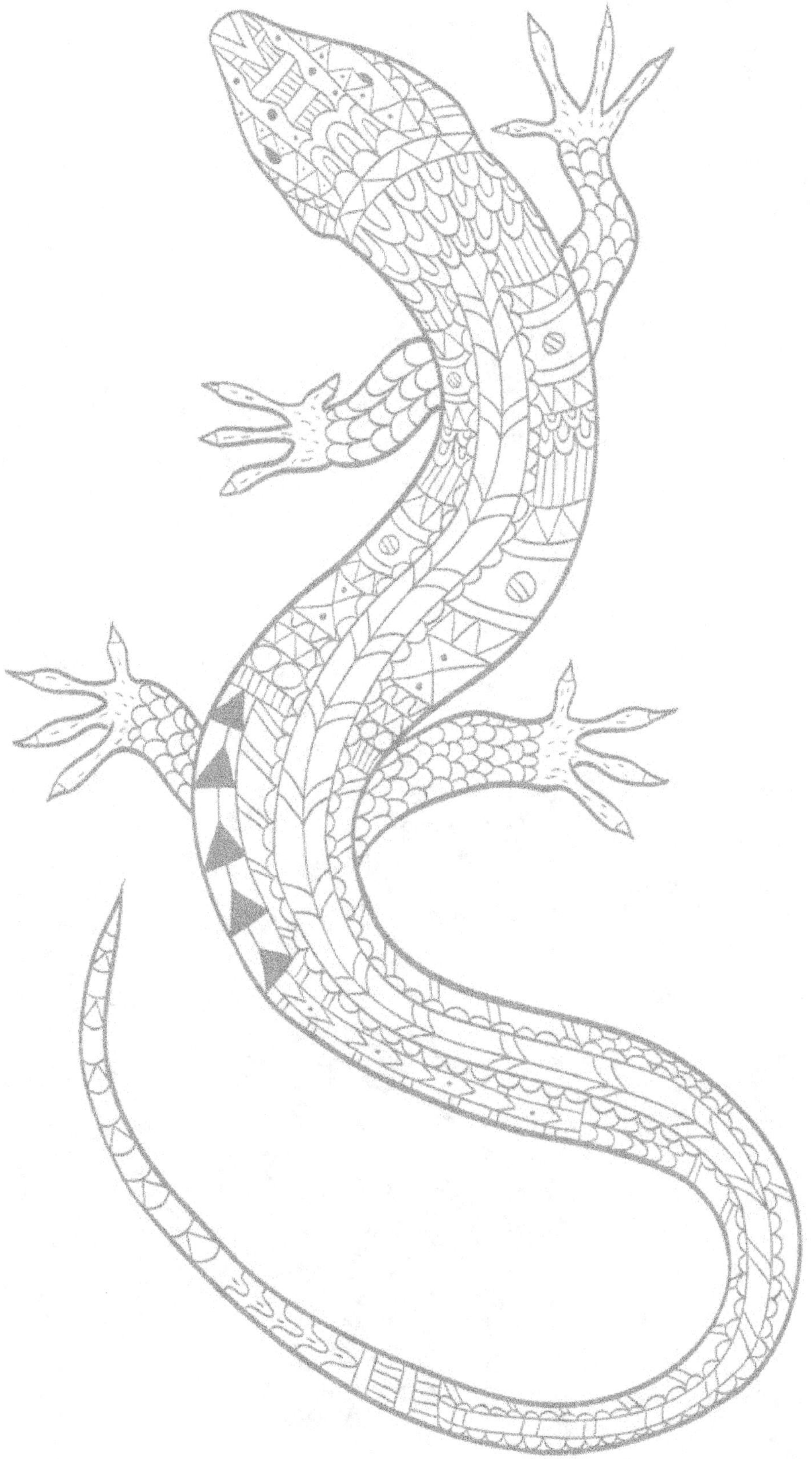

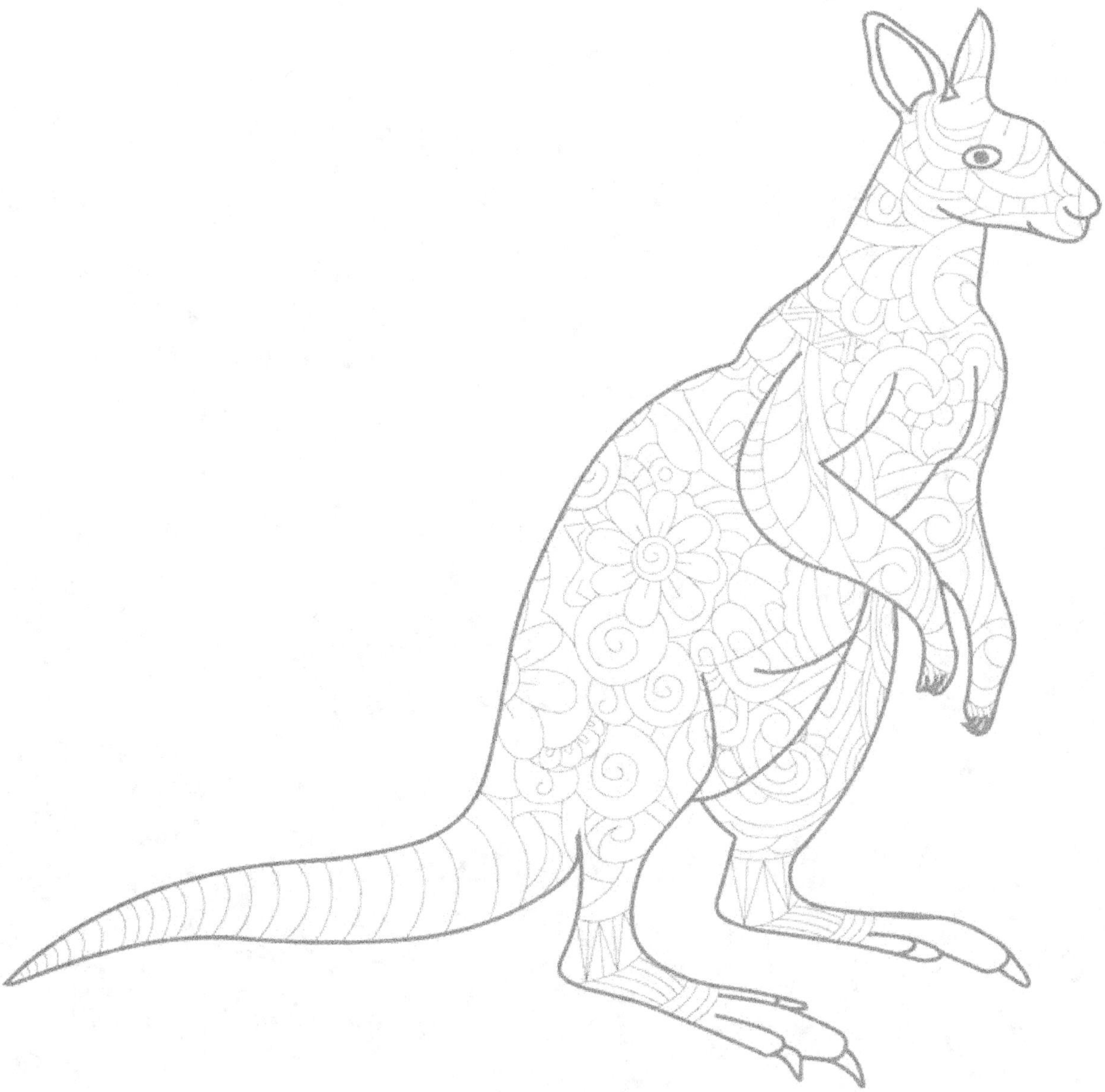

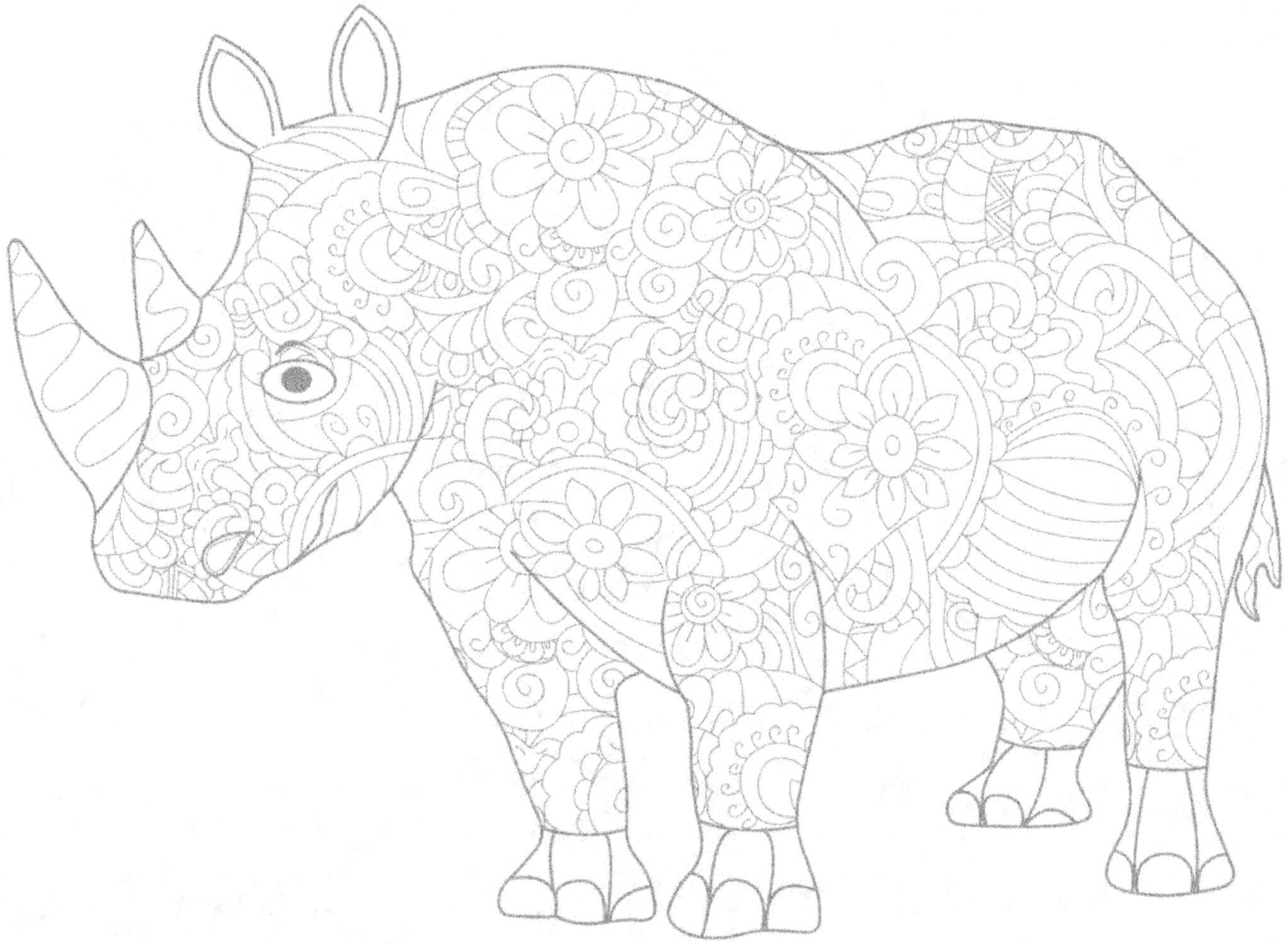

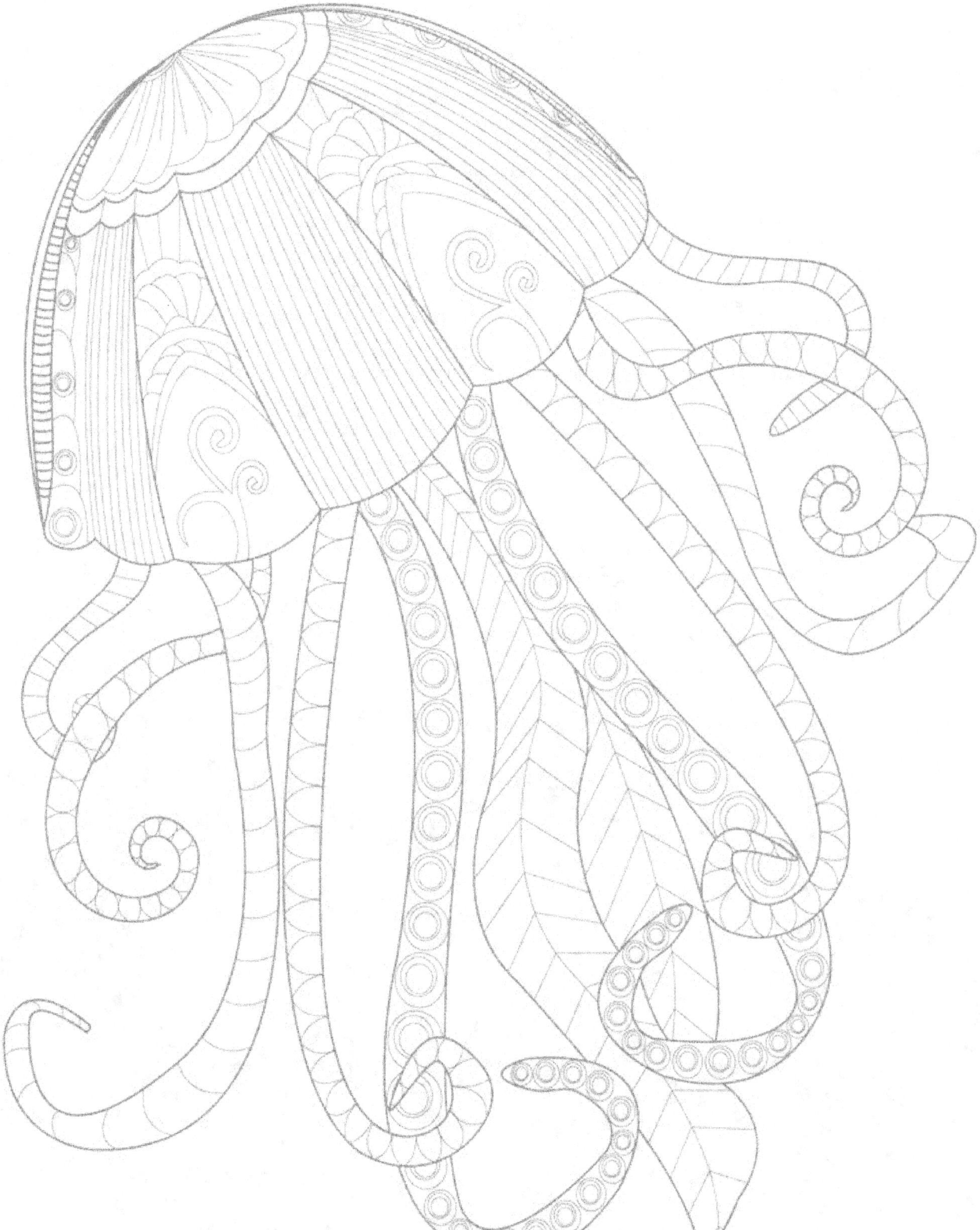

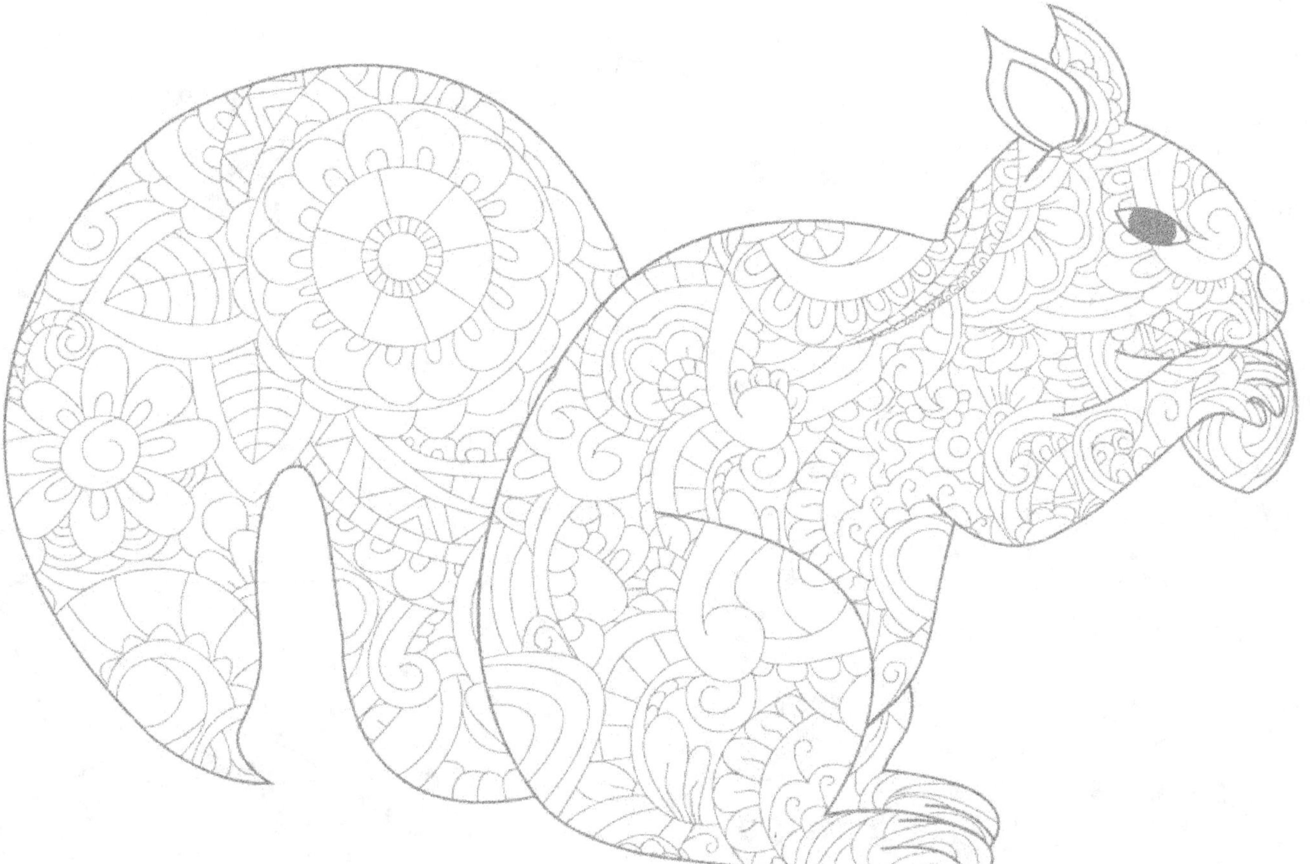

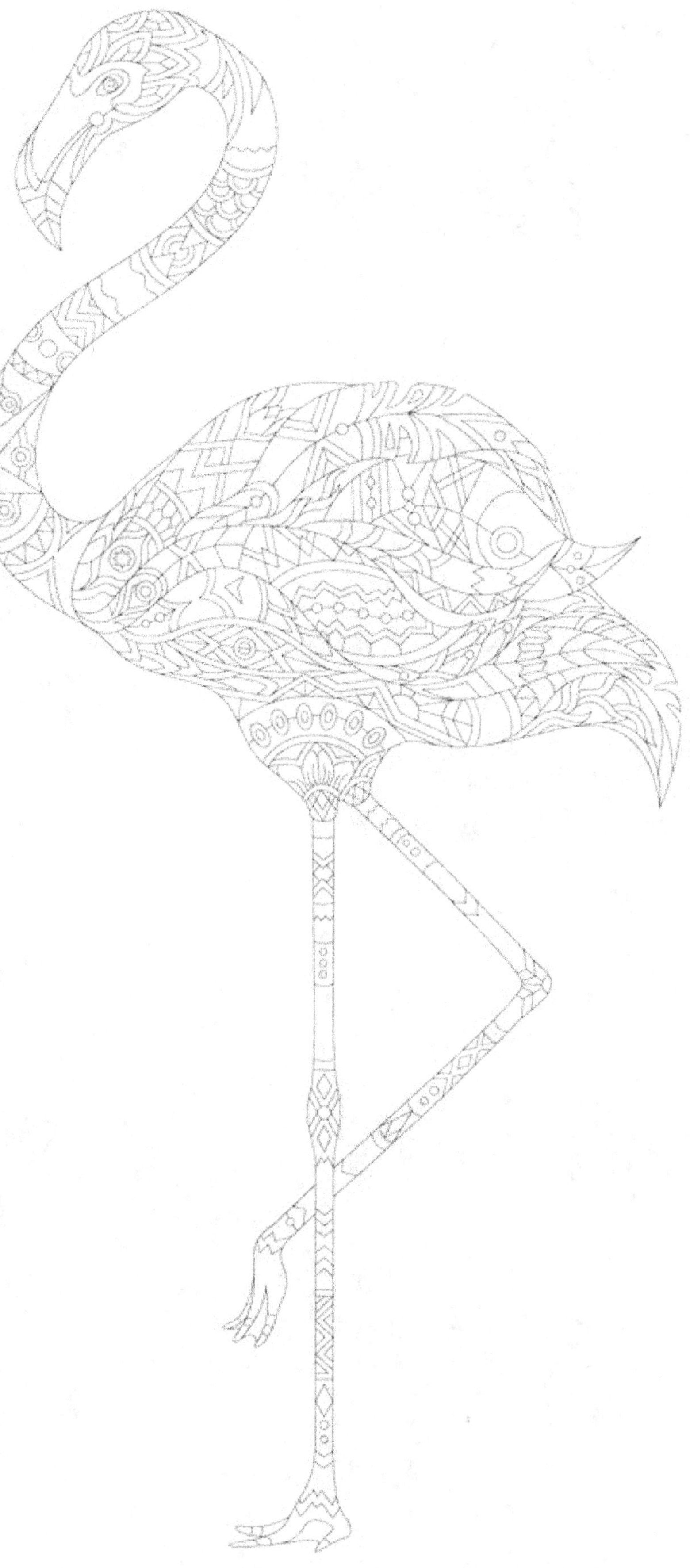

www.ingramcontent.com/pod-product-compliance
Lightning Source LLC
Chambersburg PA
CBHW081501220526
45466CB00008B/2736
9781671828155